Gifts from God
By
Cynthia Reeg

Photo Art by
MarySue Roberts

A Wings of Faith Children's Book
Guardian Angel Publishing, Inc.

Acknowledgment
To Rob, the most amazing gift in my life.

Guardian Angel Publishing, Inc.
http://www.guardianangelpublishing.com

Gifts from God
Copyright© 2007 **Cynthia Reeg**
Illustrations Copyright© 2007 **MarySue Roberts**
ISBN 10: 1-933090-33-2
ISBN 13: 978-1-933090-33-7
June 2007
Published in the United States of America

Guardian Angel Publishing, Inc.
12430 Tesson Ferry Road #186
Saint Louis, MO 63128 USA

All rights reserved

Names, characters and incidents depicted in this book are products of the author's imagination or are used fictitiously. Any resemblance to actual events, locales, organizations, or person, living or dead, is entirely coincidental and beyond the intent of the author or the publisher.

No part of this book may be reproduced or transmitted in any form or by any means, electronic or mechanical, including photocopying, recording, or by any information storage and retrieval system, without permission in writing from the publisher.

God surrounds us each day with wondrous gifts. Simple gifts. Joyous gifts. Loving gifts. As my thank you to God for all He has given me, I compiled here a short list of His bounties.

Cynthia Reeg

*I will walk among you and be your God.
(Leviticus 26:12)*

God plays above me.

I have set my rainbow in the clouds, and it will be the sign of the covenant between me and the earth. (Genesis 9:13)

God follows me.

Go up to the land flowing with milk and honey.
(Exodus 33:3)

God flows beneath me.

You are the temple of the living God.
(II Corinthians 6:16)

God lives inside me.

Shout for joy, O heavens; rejoice, O earth; burst into song, O mountains! For the LORD comforts his people and will have compassion on his afflicted ones.
(Isaiah 49:13)

God stays near me.

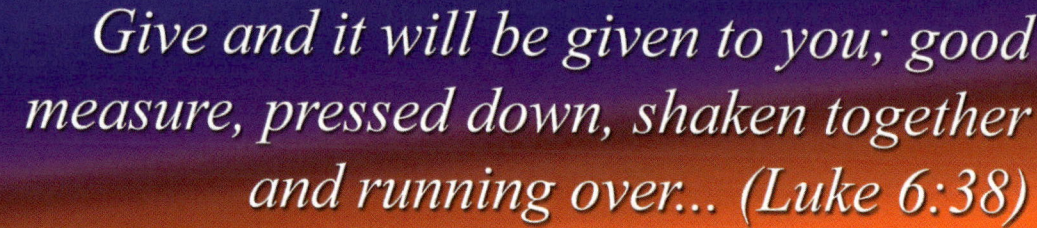

Give and it will be given to you; good measure, pressed down, shaken together and running over... (Luke 6:38)

God gives to me all good things.

Cynthia Gagnon Reeg pursued her love of reading and writing with an undergraduate degree in English Literature from Northwestern Oklahoma State University and then a Masters of Library Science from Oklahoma University. She has worked in school and public libraries throughout the Midwest.

Cynthia lives in St. Louis with her husband, Robert, but they also love spending time at their vacation home in southwest Florida. She has two grown sons, Matt and Dan, who have provided her with inspiration since they were babies. Her cats Herman and Henry, and dog Holly serve as creative consultants for all Cynthia's stories. She enjoys hiking, dancing and, of course, reading.

Cynthia is a member of the Society of Children's Book Writers & Illustrators and the St. Louis Children's Writers' Circle. Her children's writings have appeared in FACES, My Friend, Clubhouse, Dragonfly Spirit and soon in Ladybug and Highlights. She received the Missouri SCBWI's 2006 Mentorship Award.

Three of her poems have won top honors in the annual Springfield, Missouri Writers Guild Contest. Her children's book, KITTY KERPLUNKING, also published by Guardian Angel Publishing, Inc., has received rave reviews from school reading specialists and is used as a part of the OASIS tutoring program in the St. Louis area.

For more information about Cynthia and her writings, visit www.cynthiareeg.com

MarySue Roberts is an independent professional photographer/writer living in southern California.

For over three decades, her stories and award-winning images have been used in newspapers, magazines, books, corporate news and marketing and hang in private collections.

Currently she is working on a children's book and a photo documentary, illustrating the beauty of the Southwest from the high deserts, through the mountains and to the sea.

"With just a twist of creative imagery, inherited Nikons, and an absolute passion for art, my photography often reflects my abstract view of the world - without losing touch with reality," Roberts said. "It might be a liner slowly leaving port, children playing, a street corner, or my own backyard, the splendor around us begs to be captured and shared."

Roberts is a graduate of Webster University St. Louis. She is a member of the San Pedro Art Association; Palos Verdes Art Center; American Honda Photo Club; Southwest Manuscripters, and the National Association of Photoshop Professionals. Visit her online at www.byms.smugmug.com

Printed in the United States
92087LV00002B